iota Poetry

Poetry | Reviews | Features

Issue 95

Contents

Poetry

Reviews

Features

Editorial
Spring 2016   95

*i*OTA is the Templar periodical published three times each year; in Spring, Summer and combined Autumn and Winter issues. If you have created original, innovative and imaginative poetry please do submit your work to us for consideration. We welcome work by new and unpublished writers alongside those with work in print. The content of *i*OTA reflects an eclectic range of excellent writers, and we also include work commissioned from our own community of Templar poets.

Writers across genres are preoccupied with the importance of publication and the processes around submission. At a recent publishing fair in London a panel of editors and publishers addressing a group of mainly aspiring writers were unanimous in suggesting 'the letter' accompanying a submission of new work was the most important element in the process of getting work accepted for publication. No one mentioned that perhaps the work itself or its qualities ought to be considered as the sole criterion on which the decision to publish should be based.

This is not a view shared by the Templar editorial team in arriving at decisions on publishing new work in iOTA or any of our pamphlet, collection or anthology publishing opportunities. Our sole interest is in finding excellent writing and publishing it as widely as possible using our range of transmission resources. But do ensure you tell us how to get in touch.

This issue of iOTA is the first in a new format which includes an interview with Tom Weir who talks frankly about the significance of becoming published. Chris James features the poetry of winter and there is a selection of reviews.

Our Templar Poetry Live events programme gathers further momentum in the next few weeks and running into summer, featuring launches of new collections and pamphlets at Keats House, launches at The Crescent Arts Centre in Belfast in May, readings at the Belfast Book Festival in June and Ledbury Poetry Festival in July leading up to the Derwent Poetry Festival in November.

We hope you enjoy this issue and keep up with all our ongoing news on Twitter, Facebook and our e-newsletter.

A.McM.

Published in 2016 by Templar Poetry

Fenelon House
Kingsbridge Terrace
58 Dale Road, Matlock, Derbyshire
DE4 3NB

www.templarpoetry.co.uk

ISBN 978-1-911132-95-0

A CIP catalogue record of this book is available from the British Library

Typeset by Pliny

Cover Design and Artwork by Templar Design

Printed in England

iOTA EDITORIAL TEAM

Ian Harker

Christopher James

Thomas Kelly

Sarah Roby

Jane Weir

Managing Editor: Alex McMillen

SUBMISSIONS

iOTA welcomes submissions of new and previoulsy unpublished poetry throughout the year for consideration.

Please send poetry online using the Templar Poetry submission page at www.templarpoetry.com

Postal Submissions may be sent to:
iOTA
Fenelon House
58 Dale Road
Matlock
DE4 3NB

Between four and six pages of poetry will be considered for iOTA and there is no restriction on style. Poetry must not have been published online but we do consider simultaneous submission provided the work is withdrawn if accepted for publication by another publisher.

SUBSCRIPTIONS
Print Editions
Annual Subscription: Three Issue Per Year:
UK: £20 Individual & Institutions | Rest of World: £30
Single Issue: UK: £7 | Rest of World £11

E Book Single Issues available on digital platforms: £6

Periodical ISSN 0266-2922 | Print Edition ISBN 978-1-911132-95-0 | E Book Edition ISBN 978-1-911132-50-9

Poetry

Samuel Taylor Coleridge

Frost at Midnight

The Frost performs its secret ministry,
Unhelped by any wind. The owlet's cry
Came loud—and hark, again! loud as before.
The inmates of my cottage, all at rest,
Have left me to that solitude, which suits
Abstruser musings: save that at my side
My cradled infant slumbers peacefully.
'Tis calm indeed! so calm, that it disturbs
And vexes meditation with its strange
And extreme silentness. Sea, hill, and wood,
This populous village! Sea, and hill, and wood,
With all the numberless goings-on of life,
Inaudible as dreams! the thin blue flame
Lies on my low-burnt fire, and quivers not;
Only that film, which fluttered on the grate,

Still flutters there, the sole unquiet thing.
Methinks, its motion in this hush of nature
Gives it dim sympathies with me who live,
Making it a companionable form,
Whose puny flaps and freaks the idling Spirit
By its own moods interprets, every where
Echo or mirror seeking of itself,
And makes a toy of Thought.

      But Oh! how oft,
How oft, at school, with most believing mind,
Presageful, have I gazed upon the bars,
To watch that fluttering *stranger*! and as oft
With unclosed lids, already had I dreamt
Of my sweet birth-place, and the old church-tower,
Whose bells, the poor man's only music, rang
From morn to evening, all the hot Fair-day,
So sweetly, that they stirred and haunted me

With a wild pleasure, falling on mine ear
Most like articulate sounds of things to come!
So gazed I, till the soothing things, I dreamt,
Lulled me to sleep, and sleep prolonged my dreams!
And so I brooded all the following morn,
Awed by the stern preceptor's face, mine eye
Fixed with mock study on my swimming book:
Save if the door half opened, and I snatched
A hasty glance, and still my heart leaped up,
For still I hoped to see the *stranger's* face,
Townsman, or aunt, or sister more beloved,
My play-mate when we both were clothed alike!

Dear Babe, that sleepest cradled by my side,
Whose gentle breathings, heard in this deep calm,
Fill up the intersperséd vacancies
And momentary pauses of the thought!
My babe so beautiful! it thrills my heart
With tender gladness, thus to look at thee,
And think that thou shalt learn far other lore,
And in far other scenes! For I was reared
In the great city, pent 'mid cloisters dim,
And saw nought lovely but the sky and stars.
But *thou*, my babe! shalt wander like a breeze
By lakes and sandy shores, beneath the crags
Of ancient mountain, and beneath the clouds,
Which image in their bulk both lakes and shores
And mountain crags: so shalt thou see and hear
The lovely shapes and sounds intelligible
Of that eternal language, which thy God
Utters, who from eternity doth teach
Himself in all, and all things in himself.
Great universal Teacher! he shall mould
Thy spirit, and by giving make it ask.

Therefore all seasons shall be sweet to thee,
Whether the summer clothe the general earth
With greenness, or the redbreast sit and sing
Betwixt the tufts of snow on the bare branch
Of mossy apple-tree, while the nigh thatch
Smokes in the sun-thaw; whether the eave-drops fall

Heard only in the trances of the blast,
Or if the secret ministry of frost
Shall hang them up in silent icicles,
Quietly shining to the quiet Moon.

Pipistrelle

As he turned from his piss into the hedge
in the still half-light he blinked to freeze
that snap on his retina,
the predatory fetch of webbed flight

before it jagged and veered and brushed
his left shoulder. He stood and gaped.
The fly who thought she'd made her escape
tickled the back of his throat.

Shem, Ham, Japheth

The issue: after the cloven-trottering sow
and piglets' emergence from the ark
he'd looked up, taken down, measured out
and constructed — muddied, students of Bach

grunting their canon, squinting,
whining, *"This issue: after the cloven-*
trottering sow..."— and the sun bringing
the rat-like flights of hooded crows

and the rat-like flights of feral pigeons
with cross-referenced, embellished fables
of sow and growers' pellets and generations
under the eaves of stables,

after the level of the remains of the weather
had sloped off down the sloping fenceposts, fifth to fourth;
the issue here is whether
to call the child Ham or Shem or Japheth.

The Peahen

It is not, sir, your imitation of the sun
whose luminescence you filched through the blueberries,
the redcurrants, sun-ripened minor planets
sparkling with unknowable rain.

It is not, sir, your sub-DJ scratching,
your arse-first shuffling round the barnyard hens
in some hyperbola lost to science and lost
to the scales on our feet that itch
when the quarter moon's calling us to roost.

It is that there may be
an orrery of worlds
half like you in looks and half like me.
That I may be the focus and the star.

Saddlegraft

See how I hold last year's growth,
the pencil-thin scion in my left;
I'll wrap my right hand's fingers
so around the knife,

bringing thumbs together, to lock them,
to rock them, like closing a book.
If there's tension in the wee bones
to make the blade slip, or some sprite in the wood,

just start again. I'll show you how,
talking to you. This year's our first.
Later I'll lift you onto my shoulders.
You'll ask about the frozen earth,

how long trees can stand the cold,
if their roots are like metal. Or like flesh.
Cut a saddle in negative, a notch
to marry the rootstock's wedge.

Till now it was my Dad I spoke with
in my head to keep me right. You bite
off this much tape. Fit the scion
on the rootstock. Bind it tight.

The Cloud Collector

He keeps cirrus in the cellar,
stratocumulus stuffed like insulation in the loft.
Spare rooms billow with altostratus.
Outside, the sky is a cloudless blue.
He roams the hills with a Dyson and scoops
clouds from summits in butterfly nets,
bagging them on the quiet; he stitches
them into the lining of his jackets
presses them into the boot of his car.
Each summer, he rents a beach hut,
plain white, with yellow bunting hanging
above the door like a row of crows' beaks.
He watches waves curl like rolling papers
and waits for dreams to blow in from the sea.

Song of March

This is the season of the boxing hare,
the quickening of the field
and the thin gold sun on the back of a crow.
These are the waiting days; the trees
in mad March frozen in their winter poses.
Three scarecrows stand apart, a ragtag Magi,
their gifts of silence offered to the sky.
This is the season of the buck and doe
the dull greens, the clay earth browns:
the drab rainbow of the equinox.
This is the biding of time, the foreshadowing
of spring when branches of sunlight
fall on the forest floor. Listen to the pulsing
of the stream, the soft tread of the Muntjac
and the whispering of thistles in the ditches.
This is the season of the sand martin,
the wheatear and the sky full of swifts
that scatter across the moon. Listen
to the song of the hedgerows, the thorns
that circle the fields, and then the quiet
of the fox that waits at the railway crossing
for the gate to open and the world to rush in.

The Last Day of Rome

We knew the day would come.
This time we could not buy them off
with our pepper or silk or gold.
They tore open the Salarian Gate,
emptied our granaries and stood
where our gods once stood
in the arches of the Coliseum.
With the Vandals already in the city,
I took to the hills with a flagon of wine.
Behind me, Rome burned: they
scattered the ashes of our emperors.
Water drained from the bath houses;
blood spilled from the Senate.
All around me olive groves
were lit like torches on the hillside.
Cattle ran free; men lay drunk
with togas around their waists.
I ran through the old forest,
attended by a guard of flies,
and hid, while the Barbarians
took our world; one came so close
I smelled the vinegar in his beard.
His eyes were wild with spoil.
Then I saw a she-wolf watching me,
two boys suckling beneath her.

The Dove at St Peter's

We followed the dove into the ruin
of St Peter's seminary, Cardross.
Cradled by trees, hewn from light,
cast in concrete as strong as their faith,
this was the abandoned place.
The bird swept through the chapel
fluttering like a letter thrown to the wind,
the word set free. It weaved through
each arch, stitching them together.

More of a bunker than a church,
a temple of lines and light and curves,
it sheltered them from the world,
but now even the rain got in.
The dove threw its shadow across
the altar, brushing sunlight
from the steps while we listened
to the wind, rushing up like a babble
of voices into the roof and sky.

Then, distantly, we heard men singing,
their song echoing across the years;
we saw their shadows against the walls.
And in a moment the moss disappeared,
the concrete glowed white, beams
sprang back and graffiti vanished
letter by letter. Its work done, the dove
flickered up, moon-white, leaving us
standing in a miracle of wood and stone.

On a Railway Platform

Lit only with a thin cedilla moon
he measures time by shadows
falling on tracks that once
carried the finest cow-hide
raised in high country
straight to his waiting cyclamen hands.

Crouching on a rickety stool
rangy and ragged
he is an eagle
in a checked seventies suit jacket
tight on broad shoulders
that recall that great coat
he wore walking
through a Hungarian winter.

The heels of knee high boots
leaving bespoke intaglios in snow
still on distant hills
when black stilettos came
lightly dusted
with Budapest summer.
Dreaming a world before
gladiator sandals
plimsolls, pumps and puma
the shoeshine man under Cassiopeia.

No Direction Home

From Rashidiyeh camp an air-raid siren
scores southern Lebanon's graffitied sky
as Fatima sits with her back
to her shack's breeze-block wall and recalls

snow white souls of mulberry moths
and the high silvery hum
of leaves on each and every olive tree
suckling young and old on finest green-gold

grown in Galilee's dusty grey ground
with figs and pomegranates and grape vines
entwined on solid two-storey gables
bought and paid for with Palestinian pounds

saved in the tin toffee box she prises open
to show a British Mandate certificate
of ownership for a house in Um Al-Farajh
and nineteen dunums of land

taken by soldiers with scars in their eyes
and arms full of ashes.
O daughter, how goodly their tents
now a new moon scythes a meadow of stars.

The Medicine Maker

in memory of Mailya McGuigan (née Higgins)

With boneblack hair
coloured like your familiar
the sight-hound bitch
you strode the roads
eighty-seven years
(give or take a few).
Age and ache stooped spine
your business.
Straight as a seahorse
at each vehicle's approach.

Mary turned Mailya
on a grandchild's trying tongue
casting speaking stones
in a feather moon.
Your baize bag spilling
elder and hawthorn
cavorting orange rose hips
litter of gold ragwort
groundsel and brooklime
feverfew, brighteye, wild thyme.

Hung to dry in a pantry
beside blood staunching cobweb
wake candles, red flannels
small glass bottle
to draw boils
jar of forge water for warts.
No truck at all with medical men
trafficking troche and tincture
decoction and demulcent
they could not make.

Without physician or penicillin
pneumonia took you
nowhere at the end.
Taking yourself instead

as a perfect planetary day
dawned at the entrance
to the apothecary's garden.
First white petal
on the first white flower
chance mutation in a world of green.

Kicking Leaves

(A Mother's Plaint)

He'd have been thirty tomorrow,
kicking arse, kicking against pricks,
kicking a Sunday League football,
admitting he kicks himself now
for saying *No* to that lovely girl.

Leaves are falling late this year:
no quick frost to let them go.
It's called abscission, word entailing
scissors and abscess, before scar.
But today I had to cast him off,

because my winter has officially come
and ice has turned me inwards.
When Fall is finally fall I'll watch
gusts scuff a few - sun-surface eruptions -
as he used to: here, there, here again.

Tail-End Charlie

(July, 1953)

On trips out in the Standard,
Uncle Ralph made up weird stories,
one with the following characters:
Erik the Kruel, Mr E. Gregious,
and the faceless ferryman.

A dark tale, like the cloud
tracking us to Cheddar Gorge,
stalling as we dropped down
in imitation of the slip of aeons,
to a windmill-whirring hell.

Dad still had his 'Monty's hack',
rough as the nylon brush he used,
but Ralph's hair was growing out
and over his jacket's quotation marks.

'Rear gunner OK?' my mother asked.

Ralph didn't answer, just kept
drawing on the steamed-up window -
Mr G, 'the Styx', a pitiless king.

The driver's mirror was a little TV,
my father a newsreader looking anxious.

Savage God

These days they mess with gas
to betray its purer stealth,
but nought barred the hell-bent
when steel-holders swelled
from pinched to plenitude –
like miserable Jack Day
(Can a name kill with its plainness?),
eyes a pair of Winter suns,
watching the untormented crowd
file smiling past his window
before he dissolved to the kitchen.

Shopkeepers stood gagged in clumps,
firemen danced after naked flames,
and relatives bore down on May,
the widow returning laden,
who must have seen from way off
a howl in her house, opened up.

I remember his conker-shine shoes
and think of a preparedness for
something aching to become an event.

My Love for You

will not be a thing sung from rooftops. More likely,
it will be the scunch and cratt of claw in corrugated rucks
you hear. I take my breaths, my chests holds birdy-hops –

my body is the weight of a drowning cow.
Ticker-tock, ticker-tock to four o'clock, six o'clock –
what are you doing, what are you doing right now?

I have been dallying with the image of our heads
in cornflowers – I had that buzz of knowing
there was no rush, that you were going to kiss me

at some point, so we had time to watch the bees.
What are you doing, what are you doing right now?
I have sat for so long under pellum – I am the dusty bust

of Lady Blah-Blah, calico cover slipped over one eye,
offering her maudlin peeping to the snag of stucco traps.
Hello Crazy Town, I tell the face that crimps at me

like a woken werewolf – if I could leave this traitor
in her mirrored den I would. *Out! Out!* She has teeth
for tender flesh. *How are you, how are you today?*

I want to stand outside your house in pouring rain,
pool myself on the welcome mat – I could carry
the transfer of your face on my puddling. If I was snow

I could fall in flakes around you – you could catch me
on your tongue. I am the pain of uneaten berries –
I am their waste on bush. *LovemeLovemeLoveme* –

I roll my blousy battleship to bed; lay as if I am dead.
Hello, my darling comes the croon from comely meadow.
You fantasist – when did you ever talk like that?

Your Scars

I could run my finger down each one, pretend
to tell fortunes, but I am not touchy and he
is not there for the feeling. Hatchet job of keloids –
I am not looking. I am not looking, yet I am.
I see them. Slicings that make me short of breath -
woman, you're a mess. You really are –
you're a culture of pain. A fucking vampire – as if
lipping them could plug you into his darkest parts.
Stamping my feet like a small child. *I have them inside!*
Like he has only been waiting to pander me, spoiled bitch
who cannot use her usual flirts, is trying to connect to his
brick wall. *Why, even?* It's the hurts – he went nearer
to death than me, makes me a faker. I want
his hand on my chest. *Feel them!* My lines.
Ugly, fat-lump woman – here comes
your worst nightmare. Everything hurts,
every bloody moment of every shitting day.
He wrote about some girl he loved – what about me?
Everyone ought to want me more than they wanted anyone.
This is what I tell my reflection. Look at your double chin,
you deluded cow. Your pretty is over – pity
you never learned to live without the crazy.

Diving for Pearls

Escapism's rife — diving for pearls —
the world and his wife, diving for pearls!

To delve in paint, affording earrings,
the palette and the knife — diving for pearls.

For love, my stomach thinks my throat's cut —
oysters will suffice, diving for pearls.

The pearl's own auction — none had the price,
buying itself from itself — diving for pearls.

Dropping dew, the places where he passes —
thirst slaked, my life staked, diving for pearls.

An afternoon spent trying to capture
butterflies — good grief! Diving for pearls!

Amnesia induced by sunrise —
the earth forfeits strife, diving for pearls.

The Near Eclipse, Near Easter

The hedge is casting crescents to the ground –
among the greying lichen on the pavement slabs –
the branches and thorns no longer between them
direct in their absence the shapes that the light makes –
because the light, during an eclipse, keeps
its restricted nature through gaps where it shines.

The moon is the stone rolled to and from the tomb.
The stone is making what seems to be a tomb
from where the light is present. The cusp of things
is in the shadows, more assertive than they ought to be;
the hedge is viciously alive and growing darker
as the sparrows of the spirit tear back in to roost.
The dark spots on the sun are what they always were –
the rooted ends of those magnetic arcs of fire.

Earth Putting Words Into The Mouths of Puddles

Puddles the length of the lane
play 'what's the time Mr Wolf?';
sing-song *At last! To be first!* Sneaking
the colours of the petals of roses
the sun must have gobbled down.

About your cataracts – that word
you couldn't look up, couldn't find –
it means *to rise* – the causative – now you tell me –
the sun has you to rise; by stealth
you have your rising by the sun.

Mosquito

When the mosquito went to bite,
the sweat on his chest was like a lake
so it dived and skimmed then
slipped away, taking perhaps
comfort in the small-minded
grace of such spontaneous things,
and he was in his own way relieved
with the chance promoted by heat
and perspiration, although clearly
unaware of being unassailed,
so that between this pair
there was a balancing of forces which
viewed by the relative nature of things
just about crystallises perfection.

Head

There is the pick-axe head, but no skull,
all pebbles cranial though too small to
tease, and a beachcomber might at first
think it has been carried by the tide over
so many miles, but with that weight this is
dubious, even considering the shifting of
tons and tons up and down that coastline,
especially in recent high waves. It will
have been more menial – and less awful –
a handle the only missing link with its past,
rusted by sea-salt rather than blood stains,
likely left after digging holes for balustrades.

Having said that, who knows what floats
way off shore, shaft in a boat's dark hull.

Gravy

For Ray, blessed in his diminishing days,
it was *gravy* – the lingo of his contentment – but
mine is all too real, where working from Carver's other
joy of what is, it now needs throwing away. My actual
day begins and ends so oppositely, from the happy
expectation and work to make it so with such relish
to then being redundant in a moment's clarity of truth
and honesty as painful as it turned out to be: also in the
shock of the telling. That too reminds me of Ray
and his warning to keep silent – the *will you please be
quiet, please* as pure pleading when knowing the
candour of revealing is also the ending of everything.

Carver's gravy that pains me with the bliss of his ease
and mine left untouched without a word for its verities.

Particle

God knows, I acquired drag
as soon as the energy
spat me out. Though I could
still remember pico-second
speed-of-light vitality.

I think I would have
taken it, that life,
a flight which wasn't even
movement, only
signature across the sky

but then you crowded in
and there was drag
and mass, the weight
of all our gravities
the screwing up of time.

If choice was any part of it
I'd say: spare the drag. Allow
the arc away. Address me
through the abstractions,
the hypotheses, the maths.

Machines will tell you where I went.

This is the truth

There really was a careful pair of guards
who may have been in wines and beers
or may have been in household goods
and also Mr Crouch who with a friend
or on his own said simply or simply didn't say,
I bet those twats won't see, who did
or didn't go there through the wind
because he thought he recognised a mate.
The lights of evening Iceland shone through glass
on rain and coats and cars, and chasing through
the gloom our man here certainly got jumped
(whether Dilan showed the right ID or not
whoever had him by whichever arms and legs).
It's true they dragged him in by Aisle 1
after the bottle fell or didn't from his coat
after his flailing fist hit Duncan in the mouth
which may have bled or may have merely bruised
and the police came after someone (Kenny?) called.
I can confirm that things were said, that fighting
could have finished with a kicking in the balls
or maybe when he figured out the odds
and cameras caught it all although the tape
– before it disappeared at least – was clearly blank.
And it's gospel – after everyone was gone
a weary cleaner swept up broken glass
or it was kicked along by several strangers' feet
into the dark.

C-Bomb

When my son spies the phallus in the face of a Dr Who villain,
I know he has found the start, sex and end of it. Like how I spent
my fears as a kid, worrying that if this urban myth came good,
I'd one day sit down over a snake that rose from the u-bend.
Later I balked at pop psychoanalysis and took the piss, pretending
to find fallopian structures in the classics. I always got good marks.
Now I worry that the c-bomb is still nuclear and that a man
once worked a connection between my crowded mouth and
his fears of clamping during blow jobs (it wasn't on the cards)
and that science fiction is still scared of its private parts.
What I need is the eighties and a protest, a peace camp
in recognition of what brings us our ecstasy and our kids.
I'd camp out beside the deep waters where MoD submarines lie,
occasionally poking their slim, dark eyelets above the surface.

Maenads

Sometimes I'm mistrusted by husbands of friends
who suspect the nights girls spend together
when the sky's black is pitched exactly
and electric lights us animal-skinned,
and the wine leads us off and astray.
It is the way our heads tilt to press our thoughts,
the sweet sibilance oiling our gossip,
the sharp intakes from heart confessions.
As if on Dionysus' way, we each struck a thyrsus
to spring the same milk and honey.

They are right to fear our desertion.
We each cup a mirrored compact to the other's talk
of the cub-needs of suckled wolves,
of the steady lick of domestic snakes,
and of how deep and at his height
we have each seen a man lost inside us.
Closing time brings the lights awake
and both tempted by this sister mirroring;
we are thrilled at how alike:
she is just like me; I am just like her.

Josefa Menendez's Road to Nowhere

These are the two-shade futures waiting in bits outside windows
after a ten-story fall. They've been called
suspicious circumstances: hotel walls with lipstick writing,
a paper-trail too hot. He leaves scans
overnight, drinks up lager and high-speed
pornography. Tongues glitter
and emerge glittering.
Outside, high speed cars burn out on the horizontal blur.
Time-space trajectories become mystical, the strange silence
of passenger seats at night. The white noise of aeroplane engines
metres away – funny how he still sleeps, nestled nose-like
between portholes. If he looked
he'd see answers spun into the patchwork, watch them merge
with clouds and roads, webbed dimensions
suddenly clear.
But ascension lasts only a moment. Like Christ's, his eyes open.
And so they close. Come down a dead pixel,
seared into the screen.

Elegy

I read this morning the conditions of your death
in an elegy
by a friend, delivered with rain heavy
on dense earth.
It was one of those days where meaning seems painted
and pressed by a brush clutched trembling,
where even
passing cars I picture faceless, exhaust hanging low and cryptic.

Sorry it's so cinematic – how apt that, when thunder sounds,
it's miles away
and those gathered (many more
than you'd imagined)
listen twice,
binge-feeling and flickering in and out
with static in the air.

He said that, in the weeks before, you'd told him on the phone
that you loved him.

I'm glad, and like to think you had your eyes shut tight
and that somehow
he'd known to close his too. Connection has, I'm afraid,
been drafted,
but small acts like these send it home, bring you back, bring the world
you longed for
stuttering into focus for a second at least, grand film stuck
in a grand projector.
I found a photo of you together, grad-school days
or something,
glasses and long hair and I can't help but insert myself,
so I won't indict you here –

I just hope
death is all you wanted it to be: coherent, a city on a hill
of empty skulls,
bone gleaming fertile in the endless summer sun.

Marine Biology

And like wind it all came down: whitebeam and cherry-blossom, a plastic bag
in a tree. Funny
how every composition hides ten or twenty quiet urchins
pawing at dirt behind.
                              Inside,
I drink dark tea with honey squeezed from plastic bottles and think
of endings,
                 of how even gyres
have loose ends that trail like ribbons
in strong winds –
                              grab hold, and watch ospreys and gannets
circle pockmarks in seawater. There are faces
in the mudflats: mouths that blur outwards, eyes that sink
into nothing.
                       And all those years ago, they would sail through here with
lepers lashed below-deck, storm tides threading home through an opal
moon. Below these waves, reality piles like sediment,
or like pages
                 of cured vellum: words and pictures in lichen red
and rich lazuli blue plot our grinning futures. Skin
and dust
              throb in sand.
                              Dig there for answers,
and find nothing – and amongst those blue lunar histories,
know that you've done well.

Into the Wild

Do you remember the struggle beneath our window
that night as they dragged the deer over the ground
by its hooves? The way it looked up, eyes unmoved,
as the white noise of friction crackled from its fur,
as blood glistened on the road and we knelt together,
peering out, the closest we'd been in months.

Do you still hear the muffled bark of the dogs
that needed to be kicked away, too eager
to end what they'd been made to begin?
Or the sound of the deer being hacked to pieces
in the back of the village pub,
of flesh and bone being broken and torn,
a sound that stalked the air for months
like the threat of a great storm.

Bad News

So it's you— the sudden bite on the air, the extra glint in the stars,
the moon that glows like hot metal in the sky,
pitching everything else into darkness.
Maybe it's this time of year, or this strange quiet,

or the bullocks I saw charging from the window of the train,
but I've been thinking about that place, the cottage,
the cows that would appear in the woods,
the bulls that used to get loose. Do you remember the time we looked up

to find one in your garden, scoffing apples straight from the tree,
or when we had to herd the cows along your drive,
avoiding the fence I'd spent all day helping your husband to build?
I can still feel the burn in my hand of smacking their flesh,

how it ached my bones like winter. Do you remember how the bullocks
would charge the gate before we'd even entered the field,
how you'd grab a stick 'just in case' and tell me to put the dog on his lead,
even though I'd read somewhere that that was the last thing you should do,

the way I'd read that once bullocks begin running down hill they can't stop
and that in Shropshire, where we were, they'd accounted for 13 deaths
in the previous 8 years alone. But I kept quiet, did as you said,
for I was still in love with your daughter then.

Rest Room

There is no finger print reader, no six-digit security code,
I'm undone by the simplicity of a swing-door; a faulty bulb
strung up on the ceiling that flickers as if it's never held

light before. I don't know if it's the clatter of cutlery outside,
the veins that trace my arms like contours on a map,
or the fact that my silver Casio slipped the knot of my wrist

days ago, but I've been in here over an hour and still
cannot move to my feet, cannot bear anymore the thought
of the traffic, the smell of boiled meat, my starched white sheets,

the air conditioning unit above my bed that's only setting
is so cold it tricks me back home each night, leaves me waking
each morning to the shock of losing you all over again.

Tom Weir

How I Found Your World Cup Replica Adidas Football
then Lost it Again

When I found your football it had been missing for three days—
since you kicked it out of your garden and into the woods
at the bottom of the hill. It had been gathered up with all the trees

and tiny pools of water by strings of wire, rusted with age.
I noticed its pale complexion poking out from the belly of a bush.
I reached in and touched it, but was unable to get a good hold,

thorns attacking my arms like a disturbed hive
as I tried to roll it back, kneading its deflated skin like dough.
Its sheen had worn through, become spongy, weighed down

with the water that swayed gently inside.
The inner-tube quivered like a rubber-band as it fled my foot,
the smack of deflated leather stinging my skin

as I watched it head back up the hill towards your house
where it fell, suddenly slipped from view,
like a bird flushed-out and shot from the sky.

Confidante

I asked the hill what she thought of this
and she said
don't think,
just pick blackberries, let their warm
purple juice stain your fingers
and the brambles prick your wrists
and hear your own ouch of protest,
close your eyes and put your face
right into your oblong
plastic takeaway box and
breathe them in.
Then taste hawthorn berry
flesh like apple,
climb up across my curves and
watch the harvester below
fold in the rape and release
a liquid flow of seeds
down that long, improbable arm
into the tractor's trailer
and think, then,
of damsel flies mating
and do what you must do.

Vigil

A sunset rip in the sky out-reds the Tesco sign
across town, but the girl who sits
with her back to the tower takes a selfie
of her feet, flicks it straight to Facebook.
The little boy Ash tries to scoop his mother
back from the mud and grass, and that man
who isn't his father holds out his hand
because no one else does.
A firework goes up so you count it out,
reach ten before the bang and ask me
when did it happen – then, or now?
It's always happening, I say –
everything, endlessly.
You give me one of those looks
so I talk about Challenger,
that 'live' footage on YouTube,
throw in the plumber in York
who saw Roman centurions
marching through a cellar,
but your silence on the way down is the final word.
Is it then it explodes, the tourist plane
31,000 feet above Sinai? Splits in two?
I turn it over and over –
bodies, arms, legs, pieces of everything
flung across grit in the mountainous area of Arish.

Ian Harker

Goldfinches Gatecrash the Arnolfini Wedding

The Arnolfinis are concentrating on looking demure,
eyes downward, surrounded by the wealth
that has unloaded itself like bales of wool,
stacks of hay, wealth like tickertape,
wealth like the tick-tick of small stones
in a moleskin bag hanging by a paunchy side
from a Moroccan leather belt.

The Arnolfinis are concentrating on being embarrassed
by the riches – chandeliers, mirrors, small dogs –
when the goldfinches arrive one by one in a line
on the telephone wires outside the window.

The dog goes mad and Mr Arnolfini stiffens
at the noise of the dog and the noise
of the goldfinches and Mrs Arnolfini thinks
he's going to lose his temper again.
Don't move! barks Mr van Eyck, but it's too late,
Mr Arnolfini's best hat is skew-whiff, the dog
is scratching at the door to get out
and Mrs Arnolfini – already four months gone –
has given up and let go of her husband's hand and flaked out
on the bed, her dress hitched up over her bump.

Mr Arnolfini yanks the cord of the Venetian blind
and sticks his head out of the window.
The goldfinches are in good form – a handful of gold coins
flung into the street, a line of red dinner plates
looking at Mr Arnolfini quizzically as he flaps his arms
through the casement, shooing them away
like the beggars waiting for him
outside Ladbroke Grove tube station
as he stalks towards the City to forklift
crates of gold bullion into the Thames.

Mr Arnolfini is startled by the gold and black and red
thronging his head, his hatless head.
You have to come and see this! he shouts to his wife
who is adjusting her head-dress in the mirror.
Come and look at this, you'll miss it! Mr Arnolfini is grinning
like a trader at close of play, black and gold and red
flapping around his head. *Come and look at the goldfinches!*

Blue God

That first summer other boys
were tight shadows,
static at the tips of my fingers
till out of a steel-white sky
that could have been cold to the touch
came you – blue like Krishna.

No one else knew.
No one could see the cobalt stream
from under your shirt. I was hot
in a school jumper but my eyes,
closed like a corpse's, opened
and found you – dancing
if you did but know it
at the end of the sky,
at all the far reaches.

And everywhere around you abundance –
petals and filigree, water
through dry earth.
And a point of light under your hand
where all the other light started.

Roped Together

Hell, they were a tasty pairing: Mick as reachy as a gibbon,
Alan double-muscled like a Belgian Blue. Any weather,
they'd be swinging from the flakes on Stanage,
necking fry-ups down at Grindleford. At night, a lock-in
at the Moon in Stoney Middleton, a stumble to the cave to kip
then up at dawn to climb away the grogginess.

I fell off the pace and sank into an armchair far away
from the lunge and grab of the gritstone crags.
I see them when I walk the dog that way; still swinging
from the rocks like pendulums of longcase clocks.

Al lost his sight at work; the safety-guard was disconnected,
never saw the welding torch was on. He says he'll manage
cos the grit's about the touch, but Mick does all the leading now,
holds Alan on a tight umbilical. They stoop up to the edges
arm-in-arm to steady one another, lay a coil of rope
beside the buttress like a wreath beneath a cenotaph.

Damian Smyth

Swimming Up English Street With Protestants

All I did was go for a swim up English Street,
Swallowing miles of water that only looked as blue
As the Mediterranean, but that was the cerulean tiles;
Only looked to have lanes wobbling on the surface,
Runways walled by stone to keep us in order, but
Those were markings on the inside, in fact, on that ceiling
The pool floor was, to which I aspired as a collector
Of weights and rings, medals, lungfuls of worn air.
A culvert bomb a mile off, on the Ballydugan Road,
Had sent the chlorine lapping the pool walls; something
Like the wine in the Europa Hotel, thrown out when a report
Shattered the linings of Balthazar and Nebuchadnezzar,
Or might have; powder of glass tincturing the vintages.
Another element, like a holy well, full of miracles,
Once a year, pool water shared with the other school:
Whole lovely selves articulate, refracted, unbroken by surfaces,
As if we had come there to be healed and were undamaged,
Each armful or embrace pulling the known world to themselves.
There were vials of Struell water for sale in the Town Hall,
But nothing, trust me, as electric as their bodies bathed in:
New wine in new wineskins; nose-fluting mouth breathers,
Exotics from the other nations: Nubians; Shebans; sea nymphs,
Watersprites, naiads; those necessary others, from those isles
To which, though barely afloat, I've not ceased to stretch my arms:
Those still possible intervals, laps, widths, strokes, lengths.

The Coney Island Watchers

There comes a point you'd be better off elsewhere,
For all the hospitality of the shore, the cool winds;
For all that the generous tides leave crockery at your feet,
If unmatched and brought down to the water years apart.
That is what is left of empire and someone's good front room,
As if there's a village of souls sunk everywhere, and fragments
Rise to the surface in any disturbance - broken roof tiles
From a tea house, beams that bore a bridge, shiny tesserae
The beachcombers study, their footprints filling up with brine;
All that's left of the searchers or what they were looking for.
There comes a point light's gradient shifts; at once,
It's time to leave the shore to refugees of kelp and wrack,
And let what's missed right now, in homes around the coast,
Arrive like a gift at night-time, leaving no mark
But its own weight pressed face down in the wet sand,
For the momentary scrutiny of the first responders
The big guardians of the shoreline are. In the marram grass,
Keeping vigil with what remains when the old tide pulls away,
There is that hunched figure prowling the glassy sand,
Bowing oddly to the Mourne Mountains across the bay,
Shuffling from leg to leg the sodden rucksack of himself:
A heron-crane, staring out to sea - its loneliness perfect
And attributable to itself; its anonymous attention to detail
Peculiar because persistent, complete and disinterested,
With nothing to gain. No wonder it seems human, eventually;
The starbursts of its long toes, round the remains, being asterisks.

The Ballyhornan Transfigurations

After a few months they become something of an embarrassment,
The shrines at the roadside out in the country and in town,
Now unrenewed with their rotting blooms, snow globes
With figurines at prayer now unlit as the batteries falter,
And only a breeze at night making the brittle polythene rattle.
Eventually, there will be nothing at all other than rubber bands
The stems decayed within, to show the intensity of a moment
That required some gesture from the rest of us, we who survived.
But just before they do, just before there is nothing at all,
And before we know that nothing will replace this last hurrah
Of carnations or dozed synthetic floret, blanched as a seashell,
There are those moments the site is transfigured: less a location
Of remembrance and more the beginnings of a forgetting
So profound, it is in fact the first and most public act of it.
Like those great yellow chrysanthemums and daffodils
The slow-moving earthmovers are – those diggers – nodding
In the distance, far beyond luminous tape itself old and rotting,
Where sightseers or passersby or the bereaved are peering
Through the false dawn of halogen lamps spitting in the rain,
For weeks on end, at the edge of a field you could grow nothing in,
Looking for all the world like an act of memory and recovery,
Before the iron petals close over the open trenches, the treads
Pass on from the grass, the light fades after the apparitions,
But, even if the odd bulb of a skull is in fact turned over,
Looking, for all the world, as if absolutely everything is still missing.

What You Do With Your Gift

A small box beautifully wrapped,
ten green coffee beans with instructions;

Preheat oven. Place on baking tray.
The aroma that emerges shall be your gift.

And what are my gifts?

That small patch of velvet above each nostril;
barn dust, the sweetness of grain
and molasses, an oiled bridle.

Exam scripts on single desks in the school gym;
plimsoll rubber, the efficiency of ink,
the cleanliness of chalk and graphite.

What I am when I open the boot of my car:
surgical spirit, the musky malt of Penicillin,
wilting hay in the sun and milking parlour disinfectant.

What you then do with the beans
is beyond the scope of this offering.

Night Watch

Each night he leaves the bed,
his feet a heartbeat on the floor,

quickens past the gape of windows,
the convenience of shadows.

He patrols the landing, nudging open doors
observed by the sentries of wardrobes.

He knows the safe places, curtained
by duvets; the tissues, the secrets, the dust.

In the morning I feel him beside me
as though he'd never been missing.

Loosely-Coupled Systems
(after 'Rich in Vitamin C' by J.H. Prynne)

You said we were like 'syrup in a cloud';
the last spark of the evening sun had arced
pleasantly across the window pane.

We heard the loudness of traffic changing gear
while the leaves rustled, arthritically.
It did us no good; I could not compute

your words. You left in a frenzy of gestures
and I sat where I always sit, imagining sweetness,
trapped by a blur of water vapour, high

above us; a stasis barely held together
with consensus and gravity. That was us,
all over, was it not?

The Synaesthesia Procedure

I'm undergoing the complete procedure;
glitches, they said, in the old grey matter

now they've shaved me and wheeled me into the theatre
masked and tooled-up as they watch me slip under

so blossom sounds just like a choir singing
thunderstorms taste of old silver fillings

Friday is grey but Sunday's magenta
peppermint sounds like pawed sandpaper

one to a hundred's a wooden staircase
verbs smell of vinegar but nouns have no taste

guitar solos swirl into typhoons of staves
and the blood melody pulses through my veins

as I come around, objects start to resolve
at first it's a shock, or so I've been told

everything is familiar, but different somehow
when I smell the word 'flower' I smell the word flower

Revenant

Sometimes *#9 Dream*, the bay window radio,
amid airwaves, lyrics, or cafes through the day.
They carry you through the membrane.
More vivid on anniversaries, as the sick light of May
sinks like a knife through epidermis.
And a sense of close-knit consciousness,
unable to write replies on letters overnight,
letters for you to sign. As if you know
I couldn't stomach a full apparition,
you manifest where the mind can handle.

    Though is it kinder I wonder, any less tense,
when you turn the house back into a gurney,
the bed where you slept into a hoist?
I don't see the purpose, what good it does.
It's not as if those words are heard
as you lip them like bubbles undersea.
Worse, hoodwinked back to that hospital stench,
pleading again for pills to doctors,
priests, impostors, miracle workers;
witness wooden crosses, hair falling out …

    And what is it with the zombie towns we visit? —
always travelling to faraway cities, trains
without stations, cars without drivers …
Why do elders stagger about like imbeciles?
And why's grandpa and grandma strangely living?
What's the point of wails, white noise, garbled tannoys?
Maybe kinder — no more comprehensible —
than blow light bulbs on your birthday,
sure this is the place to convene, under the blanket
of my eyelids, safe among the arachnids.

Homecoming

Alighting the ninety-eight with a limp, I staggered
like an old man to the park I'd not been in
since I was five or thereabouts. There I was, weary.
A new generation of tiny feet on reins
occupied my space, as if I were a ghost.
Rain kept beading on the card I insisted on writing
and the trees were insufficient. Those words, so banal.
On a sheltered, terracotta wall, they missed the mark.

While dad was away in Beaumaris with her,
he welcomed me to a room of dust, financial concerns.
Kept awake by the low frequency hum, he'd less hair
than last time. I returned a pile of films, passed them
to his armchair, moulded to his skin. Slug trails
slavered the carpet. And to this he was blind.
Three cards made a makeshift shrine. A hard drive
entertained him. Mother — *God!* — would be devastated.

We talked about his online, Thai, she-male friend,
his neighbour sawing down his forty-foot
Aussie eucalyptus, the high school's new fence
that spoils his view from the hide;
Carl Sagan, metaphysics, whether dreams of the dead
are more than neurones firing unawares;
Liverpool transfers, government cuts, plantar fasciitis,
strategies of dealing with a conniving wife …

Outside, the window frame where she used to wash up
had the look of twelve years later.
Cotoneaster up the drainpipe left no aesthetic;
to us it was merely derelict. Together we trudged
across the diagonal path to find the absence
of WiFi, the dolmen where the cat's now buried.
Didn't even notice the nettles sting.
Impressions lined up like clothes on a line.

Then back on the bus: town scenery full of tears,
too familiar, too used by time and advance.
I went so far into it, I began to blur the difference
between this and my bad dreams:
that perhaps the night really is the light, or vice versa.
How sick the stomach when those terrace houses slide by,
the terribly white Englishness in full May sunlight,
and the slow approach of the city, the choices we make in life.

Jacqueline Kennedy's Guided Tour of the White House

The glasses are quite the prettiest,
aren't they? From West Virginia.

When dinner guests take their seats
the candelabra catch the darks

of Lincoln's frock coat in the crystal
and throw the baroque golds

of James Monroe's centrepiece
against the ceiling's perfect white.

It can crawl with extraordinary shapes:
one imagines a giant kaleidoscope

or being trapped in a Picasso.
Sometimes, here in the Red Room,

I sit at this little Lannuier table
and write my notes. You know,

I can almost hear the matron
at Miss Porter's: 'Posture, young lady'.

These chairs we re-upholstered
in Morris velvet at a Massachusetts studio:

Victorian green and Empire yellow.
My favourite piece, though, is by the door,

a Baltimore lady's desk
of sandalwood and verre églomisé.
The legs need a special Mexican wax.
I'm told it takes a thousand bees

to make an ounce. It's true,
you can fall in love with the history

as though you'll never leave.
The Roosevelt china I adore.

If a housemaid breaks a cup
it's as though something of myself

has cracked. I'm impossible for hours.
There, at the end of the East Room,

we built the sweetest stage for Casals
to play for the laureates. Someone said

he could make the air grieve. Just here,
in spring, from these upper windows,

you can see the blossom, like a cake,
on Andrew Jackson's magnolia trees.

I confess, after an early morning storm
I can't bear to look: so many petals,

all torn, clinging to the panes.
Last, and most cherished, of course,

the Lincoln bed. One thinks of him
asleep between the brushed sheets,

those bony fingers on the coverlet,
his half-smile and hollow cheeks.

Pasteur's Nursery

Jeanne Pasteur 1850-59

Observe these worms,
plump and white
on their bed of mulberry,

feasting on the leaves.
Healthy specimens,
one might think,

but note the peppering
of dots like a pox.
Soon the muscles

of their jaws will sag,
skins turn brown:
bodies that swallowed

their weight in a day
too limp to move.
Not one hatchling

in this blighted crèche
will spin a thread
of silk. Is it fungus

eats their flesh,
faeces on the shoots
that strip tissues

from the gut?
Have you ever seen
a child with typhoid,
the dreamless eyes,
rose spots on the chest
that make a father freeze?

There is nothing
you can do but watch
your daughter die.

My work is to help
these creatures
weave a cocoon

so a moth emerges.

The Limitations of Artificial Intelligence

Alan Turing 1912-54

I wanted to make a machine
that could think,
that could count snowflakes
outside the window,
gauge the weight of frost in air.

That whole winter we worked
till we lost all sense
of seasons, rooms hot
as circuits hummed,
cables alive with the rush of numbers.

Soon it would match a master
at chess, measure corpuscles
in blood, the hormones
it takes to shape a gland.

Our machine became famous,
and so did we.
They called us the men
who built a brain.
And so we did. But then

it couldn't feel
a hand on the pillow,
smell soap on a towel,
taste the crispness
of a breakfast apple

or unplug its own wires
and switch off for ever, like love,
the current running through its coils.

Reviews

The Cartographer Tries to Map a Way to Zion
Kei Miller
Carcanet, 2014

Kei Miller appears to be a gifted cartographer. After a reading of poems taken from his previous collection *A Light Song of Light,* Miller was invited to talk about process. He described a period of a year, maybe more, when he would not write. Then when – through fear or force – he returned to writing, he described knowing from the start what a collection was going to 'be about' and how it was going to 'look'. Inevitably, the artificial context of an audience Q&A can reduce a more mercurial process to something more pedestrian. However I was struck by how deliberate his method and curious about the result. Miller's response is of interest here as the book he had mapped ahead of him was his current Forward Prize-winning collection *The Cartographer Tries to Map a Way to Zion.*

This collection begins with several stand-alone poems where the landscape is prone to 'fidget'. In 'The Shrug of Jah', the poem takes a kinetic sway from left to right margin and reminds that 'the world was unmapped. / In the long ago beginning'. These poems prove fluid slip roads to the collection's title sequence, which is both duel and dialogue between two characters, a cartographer and a rastaman, where the debate is mediated by a series of prosaic poem titles. The cartographer's scientific approach - to pinpoint, notate and impose control - meets with the rastaman's informed suspicion. Here the writing is nimble between dialects:

> *it's all a Babylon conspiracy*
> *de bloodclawt immappancy of dis world –*
> maps which throughout time have gripped like girdles
> to make his people smaller than they were.

As the debate rumbles, both coordinates become less easily fixed within the neat hug of their parentheses. The rastaman is challenged by science; the cartographer is captivated by Zion. This uncertainty is found in the final lines of several poems where the metre becomes a half-measure, only reaching across part of the established line length. Meantime, there are interruptions from a number of prose poems, sparky square pit stops, which explore Jamaican place names. 'Me-No-Sen-You-No-Come' translates 'do not enter/without invitation' by recasting Goldilocks as rampant colonialist:

> For consider the once-upon-a-time
> adventures of rude pickney answering to name
> Goldilocks – nuff-gyal, self-invited into house of bears,
> assumed at once her colonial right to porridge, to beds
> and to chairs.

While 'Shotover' unravels a tale of rebellious slaves, attacked by their trigger-happy master, to find a slip in pronunciation: 'Shotover - so named because our people, little acquainted/with French could make no sense of *Château Vert.*'

The press towards reconciliation offers some straightforward conclusions. Nearing the end, the cartographer points out that both sides own a bias ('every language, even yours,/is a partial map of this world'); while the rastaman scuppers the cartographer's intentions ('My bredda,/you cannot *plot* your way to Zion'). These are ideas that might be readily assumed from the outset. They are the kind of ideas that might have been planned ahead.

From here, the narrative lifts from the rational to the spiritual. In the two final poems, the rastaman gives a sermon and then a benediction in which he hopes to confer

> upfullness – as if it was a thing that could be stored
> in the tank of somebody's heart, so that on mornings
> when salt was weighing you down, when
> you feel you can't even rise to face Babylon's numbing work,
> you would know...

Given that the rastaman might have been presented clinging to the grievances that map Jamaica's tortuous history, this narrative shift is gracious. This collection offers a gentle militancy. It offers poems that can laugh, spike or bestow a 'heartbless', whatever their metre of measure.

SARAH ROBY

Moontide

Niall Campbell
Bloodaxe, 2014

The poems in this skilful and assured debut collection take deep
soundings from nature. Campbell's is tuned into its wavelengths and
strange atmospheres. Like Brontë's moors, Frost's rural New England or
Wordworth's Lakeland, his South Uist landscapes and seascapes inflect
each of his poems. He uses pathetic fallacy to build emotional intensity: the
moods of the sky, the distracted behaviours of animals, birds and even the
disconcerting power of inanimate objects. Yet the voice is feather light –
there is no sense of the ponderous nature poet here.

'Grez, Near Dusk', is almost a love letter in the manner of William
Carlos Williams:

> Just a postcard to say not that it has rained
> But that it smells impossibly of rain/
> Moths feed on this silk hour

It's an evocative sketch of Celtic twilight, a sensory map of his
emotional state where senses become intermingled: the 'bowed sky is
heavy/ with the deep song of the failing colour.' It feels painterly not only in
its title, but its effect, but it is the colloquial voice ('Let me explain how . .
.' 'and yet') that gives it its accessibility and allows the reader in.

The sea is a constant presence. It is both guardian and adversary,
but also offers surprise and renewal. Objects are washed ashore of unknown
provenance, with a mystery and purity that endows them with magical
properties: 'Ship green/ or church-glass clear - such envelopes/ of sea mail.'
In 'Sea Coins, Scottish Beach', the currency is: 'sweet, burdened trader;/
purged of its minting date, its monarch.' It is treasure from an unknown
country, which could also be a way of describing Campbell's poems.

Already some of these poems feel like they could be anthologised;
'Walking Song' and 'Song for Rarity' are infused with a wisdom, a kindness
and a universality that make them small poems for big occasions. The latter
is a litany for a wedding: 'May you find pearlriver blooming/in your garden'
. . . 'May your bed be made of blood oak,/and may you love well.' It has an

echo of fellow Scotsman John Martyn's beautiful song 'May You Never' and the air of secular blessing. Yet it is never platitudinous, rooted in fresh and unexpected detail.

The rain is an inescapable feature. To paraphrase Billy Connolly, in Scotland it's not bad weather, it *is* the weather. It is in the fabric of all things, a backdrop to all transactions, and silver-plates the landscape. Music and the idea of the song are also a key feature. Songs, whether made by the poet, the birds or wind are sacred things; they carry the spirit of the people.

Perhaps my favourite poem in this collection is 'The Tear in the Sack', which attempts to capture different perspectives and chance parallels: perhaps the overarching theme of the book. He observes how 'a nocturnal bird, say a nightjar,' sees 'with a twin perspective' – an eye on each side of its head. The voice, again, is quiet and speculative. At once the bird sees grain spilt from a split sack and 'with the other, the scattered stars.' The form - two stanzas of five lines mirrors the subject, but its brevity belies the enormity of idea. It conveys the concept of a simultaneous universe - where a thousand million things happen in the same second. While we are preoccupied with the minutiae of our own lives: 'the grain spilled on the roadway dirt'; new stars are formed, others implode. The parallels between the grain and the stars is beautifully done.

Moontide is lyric poetry of the first order; Campbell's feeling for nature has echoes of both Hughes and Heaney but the world he has created is all his own; it is a dour, rain swept Eden of inquisitive birds and tentative human relations. Above all, there is a sense of newness, renewal. I enjoyed this collection enormously and will return to it, I think especially on rainy days.

CHRISTOPHER JAMES

Kim Kardashian's Marriage
Sam Riviere

Faber & Faber, 2015

Ventriloquy as Self Defence

Sam Riviere's debut *81 Austerities* began on the internet, as a blog, and went on to win a Forward Prize for best first collection. His latest book didn't exactly begin there; it's *made* of the internet: it consists of found poems, or poems made of found material that Riviere has brought together to form 72 poems. They are divided into eight sections corresponding to the tenets of Kim Kardashian's makeup routine – hence the title.

Within these Stations of the Cross for Our Times are nine sets of eight poems each (american; beautiful; girlfriend; grave; ice-cream; infinity; spooky; the new; thirty-three) with eight further corresponding words (nine if you count 'hardcore', which at one point, aptly enough, replaces 'beautiful') making up titles such as 'american berries' and 'infinity weather'. The tick of algorithm generates the names of the poems, and, by extension, the subject matter.

That subject matter is an ordering of fragments from the biggest mass of information ever assembled, samples of pack ice brought out in blue-white cylinders, the placing of certain specimens in isolation for observation, dissection, illustration. We've become so good at blocking out words and images waving for our attention (clickbait, pop-ups, memes) that ordering a series of examples in order to emphasise how neurotic and demanding the internet is could be a form of defence.

So far so good. The thing is of course (happy freaks of algorithm aside) that it's the individual human poet that produces what we (generally) agree to be poetry. Riviere has selected and edited to one degree or another – the words in the poems aren't random; and they are sometimes, in a traditional poetry sense, effective:

> spooky pool
>
> This peeling facade was once the grand entrance
> to a long-gone attraction in what is now a slightly
> beautiful light at the end of the day, Saturday.
> The lights will be dimmed for atmosphere swims.

The longest poem in the book 'the new heaven' (which feels more deliberately managed than the others) has pace and pregnancy. But a concept-album book like this (like conceptual art and remakes of the Sherlock Holmes stories) is always going to split people up into two groups. Someone who wants the rewards of poetry written entirely by a human being will put the book down in the shop, or ask to exchange it for something else, or give it to Oxfam. On the other hand, someone who enjoys the accidents of language and the weirdness thrown out of the net like radiation will most likely enjoy it. Which you are depends on whether poetry is an escape from gaping WiFi madness, or whether taking the internet's words and spitting them back is a release in itself.

IAN HARKER

---

physical
Andrew McMillan
Cape Poetry, 2015

Tab Keys and Spacebars Aside

However permissive we may have become over the last fifty years, prudishness prevents us from writing and appreciating poems about erections as fully as poems about, say, sunsets. Even if two poems, one about a hardon and the other about daybreak, were equally well written, it'd be all too easy to go into raptures about the latter and snigger at the former.

This is the Forster conundrum. EM Forster was openly homosexual to his close circle of friends. At least half a dozen of his surviving short stories (plus a novel, *Maurice*) have explicitly gay themes. Only published after his death in 1970, some sixty years after many of them were written, people wondered if this master of English prose had run out of ideas after *A Passage to India* was published. He was *writing* plenty, of course; he just couldn't publish it. Indeed, *A Passage* could be read as Forster confronting and condemning the bigotry and hypocrisy that affected him so directly.

It affected his writing too. Even in the knowledge that a story might never even be read by anyone else, let alone published, Forster was often uncertain whether he had attained his own very high standards. In terms of explicit content, we'd hardly blink an eye at them toady ("a muscle thickened up out of gold" is about as direct as it gets); but Forster has his doubts that he is writing as well about love between men as about lives of the families of *Howards End*. He notes in his diary:

> Have this moment burnt my indecent writings or as many as the fire will take. Not
> a moral repentance, but the belief that they clogged me artistically. They were writ-
> ten not to express myself but to excite myself, and when first – 15 years back? – I
> began them, I had a feeling that I was doing something positively dangerous to my
> career as a novelist. I am not ashamed of them…It is just that they were a wrong
> channel for my pen.

Again in 1964, he remarks of a story that he tore up: "It was a
craftsman dissatisfaction that destroyed it." We are still wrestling with this
problem – how to write about sex well, and make it beautiful.

Andrew McMillan's first full collection is a part of this ongoing
struggle. He's a man writing about loving men: in spite of the increasing
parity of civil rights, this is still too rare. But he isn't just writing callow
poems about how so-and-so is really fit and doesn't know he exists. He gets
under the skin of what sexual desire is.

We don't receive a brown envelope on the first day of puberty
assigning us one of the letters of an ever-lengthening acronym. What, and
who, we desire is bound up with, comes out of, who most fundamental-
ly we are. The gay man, more conscious of his sexuality because he is in a
minority, is ideally placed to analyse what straight people take for granted.
So the poem 'Schoolboys' plunges the reader (gay or straight) back to when
sex started:

> the boys let go
> and start their conversation up again
> one puts his hand between the cheap trousers
> of the other   the way schoolgirls often
> hold hands on their way to class […]

Unsurprisingly for someone from Barnsley now living in Manches-
ter, *physical* is Northern; or rather the poems take place in the North; they
take the North as read and self-evident, but they don't make a song-and-
dance about where they are happening. Yorkshire is as messy and complicat-
ed as anywhere else. The same poem takes place not long after the death of
Margaret Thatcher, and much of Northern England is putting the flags out.
The twelve-year-olds in the poem don't see the point of setting fire to a
doll, but their teacher

> [...] stares out the window   maybe thinking
> of her son   by now a man   she goes red
> she focuses on a headline   *rising*
> *unemployment lack of manual jobs*
> the boys move seats   two others wrestle
> to impress the girls   the boys sit closer
> than they need to   the lady burns

There's so much going on in this one stanza that might sum up the book. The teacher goes red – because of the wrestling boys, at the thought of her son (who has himself become a man), and because of what Thatcher did to the community he has since grown up in. Many different meanings swing together all at once, and each reading is equally possible. Both she and Thatcher are the burning lady of the last line. And of course the boys wrestle "to impress the girls" at a time when they find "the body still comical rather than alluring"; but never the less "the boys sit closer / than they need to". Ellipsis on ellipsis.

Thom Gunn is an almost-living, almost physical presence through-out the book, and his influence on the poetry is described as "the two opposing wheels of voice":

> sleep with Thom night after night
> open at the spine   face pushed deep
> there've been times I've woke and put my arm around
>
> a pillow halfdreaming it was you

The presence of an older, also gay, man may well have helped to give the poems their assured but still-wondering tone. The book has its faults. McMillan uses the tab key rather than punctuation to indicate stress, intonation, and pace; and I'm unsure whether this is refreshing or irritating. The same is true with his love of cut-and-shut words – 'shortflightstopover', 'strengthofbody', 'movingloopingringroad'. And some of his lines would be banal if not read in a suitably pregnant 'poetry voice':

> on the floor   there are days
> when I don't miss you   or even love you
> that much   anymore

Tab keys and spacebars aside, McMillan has moments of poetic intensity that you remember, both as words and as image, long after you've

put the book down, as in the poem 'Leda to her Daughters'; and this, from
the long poem 'protest of the physical':

> something of a naked man and fire
> which is prehistoric   which is horrifying
> to be undressed so quickly   someone looking on

>   empty gallery of

silence

>   lines we cannot

cross

>   the naked flame   the burning boy

>   IAN HARKER

Pilgrim Tongues

Cliff Forshaw
Wrecking Ball Press, 2015

Consolations On the Road to Nowhere

The title of Cliff Forshaw's expansive, invigorating collection sets out the
stall. *Pilgrim Tongues* is a travelogue through geography, history and principal-
ly, language. His themes range from town planning to human immolation;
his cityscapes veer from Hull to Saigon and Jerusalem. It is a dizzying, noisy
world tour viewed through the prism of classical learning and told with
dazzling accomplishment and technique. The poet is a collector of words
and phrases, sounds and images. With a voice that is frank and inquisitive, he
tackles complex themes and ideas with enviable accessibility and wit.

It is a book of journeys, most often circular and not always satisfy-
ing. The zen-like opening lines perhaps best describe the prevailing philoso-
phy:

> You are to wander,
> Entering and departing strange villages.
> Perhaps you will achieve nothing.

The destination is not always the goal and the answer is rarely to
be found there. The consolation is in the found image, the sudden shock-
ing moment that helps interpret the world. In 'On the Road', which self

consciously apes Kerouac's staccato prose, the opening line unfolds from the title:

> (On the Road)
> To Armageddon black sunflowers hang their heads.

Fascinated, he and his fellow passenger stop the car to investigate the 'dark choked faces'. They identify the killer like detectives in a film noir: 'Fungus. None the wiser'.

Forshaw is alive to the changing language, and if he does not approve of what he himself dubs 'the oddly modern phrase', he faithfully reproduces it on the page. He hears such modernisms as 'size-zero,' 'gap-year' and 'carbon offset,' every bit as grating to the ear as Hull's 'toadish halls' are to the eye. His strategy to incorporate such banality in his verse is to juxtapose it with his vivid lyricism:

> Texas, Homebase, B&Q
> and further beyond
> where Spurn's thin, bird bone of sand
>
> drifts in from the east

The 'cut-price crowd' comes in for some scrutiny: 'coordinating between hand and mouth, phone and fag/something flaky from Greggs/that awful pie.' He harks back to a more elegant age: the postie with his bag 'worn soft by hands to something approaching silk' to the current incarnation of the postman with his Hi-Vis vest and 'iTuned shaven head.' Yet he rarely judges, merely showing what we have become – a consumerist crowd that has somehow misplaced our sense of beauty.

When thrown into other foreign landscapes – Israel this time – he finds himself suddenly a stranger to language. He finds it, by turns, frustrating, beguiling and intoxicating. It is a familiar feeling to those who love language and suddenly find themselves perplexed by words they cannot understand. He confesses: 'I'm foreign, speechless, dumbstruck, mute.' And yet he begins to piece it together, word by word, seduced by the sound of 'Alef, Kaf, Yod' and the way they 'fit to tongue.'

While his subject matter can at times be onerous, Forshaw's humour is always welcome. He has a light touch, both in his choice phrase-making, admiring the way 'lizards skedaddle' and in skilful technique

72

such as the personification in Megiddo Junction, where he notes how successive invaders: 'Slid their arms/around Israel's impossibly tiny waist.' His use of the line break here is masterful and typical of his technical control throughout the collection. The irreverent haikus which appear as codas to some of the poems are also worth seeking out; they are party pieces the poet is unable to resist showing off after a pint or two.

Some of the finest pieces here however are also the most personal, such as the tribute to what feels like his father in 'Under Travelling Skies'. He addresses the poem directly: 'You'd hardly recognise some streets, though other streets would take you back/between the bombers and planners.' It is full of knowing nostalgia for an older world of streets with a 'Co-Op/nuzzled by pub' and corner shops that 'slice corned beef.' The past is expertly conjured, while avoiding easy sentiment, the final echo of the past (and the theme of journeying) arriving in the time honoured child's cry: 'Are we there yet?'

Other journeys are doomed or filled with foreboding, as in the strange, luminous tale of a newly-wed Inuit couple who arrive, fittingly, on the whaler, 'The Truelove'. They are strange 'honeymooners stuck in Hull,' which, as they succumb to disease, swiftly becomes their hell. Elsewhere there are Homeric overtones, as in Pilgrimage to Cythera, where we hear the protagonists 'drag rowing boats across the shale.'

Pilgrim Tongues is a rich, densely populated collection that speaks to the mind and the ear. The poet is on a continual journey in search of the phrase, the philosophy, the word or the sound that will unlock the past and reveal the path into the future. It is multilingual and peripatetic in its concerns and Forshaw is always open to the strange and new. Above all this collection is characterised by an iridescent lyricism amid the garishness of modernity. Few others would notice how 'a dragonfly shimmers on the aerials' stamen.' As for the dilemma of whether to travel or stay put; between the journey and the destination; of choices made and regrets harboured, he invokes Frost with an appealing resolve: 'Forget the road not taken; you're on this path now.'

CHRISTOPHER JAMES

Byssus
Jen Hadfield
Picador, 2014

From its beguiling title, to the unusual and pleasing shape of the book itself,
Jen Hadfield's *Byssus* is like little else in contemporary poetry. By turns
luminous and baffling, Hadfield's studies of the language and nature of her
adopted Shetland are deeply original, quirky and sometimes oblique.

There is as much experimentation in form as there is in language.
Poems range freely across the collection. The lines of 'The March Springs'
for example, fall down the page:

Running downhill t

o the cockle beds

Unusual line breaks like these, even in the middle of words, bring
a sense of dislocation and mirror the fractured landscape, as well as a sense
of light and space. The free-form lyricism of the first section in this poem
is then sharply juxtaposed with the rigid paragraphs and prose poetry of
the second and third parts. If it's not too grand a comparison, the different
forms, shapes and voices, the changes in tone and pace are a little like Eliot's
ground breaking experimentalism in 'The Waste Land'. In 'The Puffballs',
the words even shrink and grow before your eyes. It's utterly unpredictable
and it gives the book a thrilling instability. The language and phrase making
is as startling as the 'skylarks going up like flares.'

The sense that everything is alive – that nature has a consciousness
– is another motif. Cockles have 'a brackish smile' while the 'lichen listens'
rather like the 'thousand mushrooms' that 'crowd to a keyhole' in Derek
Mahon's 'A Disused Shed in County Wexford'. One of the most successful
poems in *Byssus* is also one of its more conventional, although even this has
a trick up its sleeve. 'The Black Hole', about a cat stalking the corpse of a
dead blackbird, is an imperfect sonnet of 13 lines, the loss of a line perhaps
reflecting the loss of life (or maybe 13 signifies the unlucky talisman of the
dead bird). In something of the style and manner of Ted Hughes, Hadfield
brilliantly captures the essence of both creatures: the stiffened blackbird
'thickly leaved like the pages of a burnt book' while the cat 'teeters/on the

brink.' His 'flanks palpitate' as he stares into the abyss of its 'eye, a scuffed sequin of blood.' It also has echoes of Keith Douglas' 'The Sea Bird', and is similarly magnificent.

There is a strong vein of humour running through the collection, which prevents it from taking itself too seriously. She reflects: 'If my kidneys complained, they were Bert and Ernie.' Meanwhile, in 'Revolution Politics Become Nature' she talks of 'the shadow cabinet of seals.' Sometimes titles are disarmingly informal: 'We climb the hill in the dark and the children are finally given back their iPhones.'

Hadfield has a Muldoon-like fascination with new words and the naming of things. In 'Lichen', 'the little ears prunk,' while elsewhere there is 'a ripened copepod', there's also 'squill' and 'byssus' itself (the mussel's 'beard' – the fibres that allow it to attach itself to the sea bed.) It adds to the sense of newness of the place and the vitality of the language is a reflection of the natural world. She coins new words and phrases – the kenning-like 'app-light' is particularly effective.

For all its dazzling accomplishment, it was an occasional frustration of Ted Hughes' work that his subject matter was weighted so heavily in favour of the animal kingdom. Here, Hadfield explores both the natural world and human relations. My favourite poem combines the two: 'You were running a bath and being Gulliver' is full of intimacy and displays an absolute mastery and control of language:

> – on your index finger was a moth . . .
> whose nano-drag on the ball
> of the digit
> was the weight and heft of a pheromone

The delicacy of the imagery and feather light touch is as impressive as her phrase making: the moth:

> tacked its invisible crampons
> into your fingertips mazed whorls

while it shivered 'the eloquent flakes of its wings.'

In its originality and experimentalism, its magical lyricism and boldness of form, *Byssus* reminded me of Matthew Welton's work. However,

I can't think of many other poets who are writing this well in Britain today. When I first picked up this book I was wary of its indulgence and disregard for convention, but in the end was entirely seduced by its colloquialism, its breathy assonance, its strangeness and beauty. She presents her adopted Shetland, its language, nature, customs and people through a new and powerful lens.

CHRISTOPHER JAMES

Night Letter

Fiona Moore
HappenStance, 2015

Night Letter follows Fiona Moore's first pamphlet *The Only Reason for Time* (HappenStance, 2013), originally featured in the Guardian. Her debut focused on her grief following the death of her husband, and poems in her new collection continue with that theme. These poems are powerful, communicating loss in their tender and subtle form. In 'The Embrace' she recalls a lucid dream where she sees, touches and talks to her lost partner. The poem emphasises the dislocation of such dreams where we are simultaneously present and absent.

> We wanted to lie down together
> but there was no time
> so we agreed to meet
> later.

In the closing lines of 'The Embrace' the ambivalence of feeling glad to have seen the person while also feeling their loss almost completely afresh when waking is tangible. The quiet technical craft of Moore is shown in this poem as well, with the halting voice created by the irregular line breaks reminiscent of someone trying to recall a dream before it fades. Similarly, in 'Limehouse' the structure is more covert than a poem with a strict formal layout. Yet it is present in her steady repetition of water and river throughout, and of phrases whose meaning is gradually amplified.

> is it you following me, or I you –
> your likeness slipping away
> A shadow on water?

The night is a time when we can no longer distract ourselves and our unconscious mind is left to roam, and so it is a time when grief has free reign. The title poem 'Night Letter' is very much about the raw experiences of loss, and along with 'Limehouse' and 'The Embrace' these poems have a natural affinity. It is a reminder of the importance of pamphlets, bringing together poems that might otherwise be spread singly between different poetry journals. There is a raw feeling channelled into all of these poems. They show us how 'Each sleep/ interlocks with the next' in a powerful unfettered landscape, and which has a parallel reality of its own, charged with emotion which is the unconscious partner of the one we also live in the waking world.

TOM KELLY

Only by Flying
Helen Evans
HappenStance, 2015

We Have Lift Off

Only by Flying is Helen Evans's debut pamphlet, and many poems are inspired by her experience of flying gliders. Poems like 'Vantage Point', express a sense of freedom and being separate from the world as we go 'towards the light, up through the gap, and out'. Others show us that flying can be a real challenge and that as well as being an escape, it can be 'faltering and bumpy'. But we spend just as much time on the ground as we do in the air, as Evans carefully provides us with contrasts throughout the collection. The poem about a day when she could not take off, 'Grounded', is just as central to the collection when the promise of getting back into the air is just as important as actually being up there:

> Even when I'm holed up in my room,
> believing I'll never fly again,
> I keep on checking the sky.

As one might expect from a collection about flying, there are several poems that feature birds – wrens, doves, dippers, sparrow hawks, goldfinches, and kites and many lines in these poems are sharply original. 'Leave-Taking' is particularly poignant. In it, we watch as a red kite executes a sombre fly past at a pilot's funeral. Those who have seen red kites will recognise the careful observation here as we imagine that big wedge-shaped tail remaining static, for once, out of respect.

77

No acrobatics.
No fancy flicks of the tail.
No thermalling away
from the hill.

In 'Edgeing' birds echo the flight of gliders as we find them 'climbing and diving/ wheeling and rising' through the air, these 'bird poems' help to ground the collection. In 'The Dipper at Rooksmoor Mills', flight is no liberation for this little bird who must live in an earthbound world where she builds her nest 'in a wall by the A46'. Similarly, the wren in 'Fledging' is watched closely by a cat who, we surmise, has taken most of her chicks already. This is certainly not overly-romanticised nature poetry, and is the stronger for it.

There are some weaker elements. 'Search Engine' seemed to be an overly self-conscious effort at the modern in a collection where the man-made and the natural are otherwise seamlessly merged. "'I' realises he is a romantic lyricist' is a poem about writing poems, and this poem is held in sharp contrast by the sheer scope of the other poems in the collection which offer such a panoramic view. Alongside poems like '*Yet I will wait for the light*', a poem about an archaeological dig provides poignant perspective on life and time in only 34 words, "'I' realises he is a romantic lyricist' seems small despite its length. But these are minor deficiencies in this skilled debut. The final poem reminds us that, no matter how great the wordsmith, we must experience some things in our own skin in order to fully understand them, some things that we can know 'only by flying'. This is a collection which will encourage you to get into the cockpit yourself.

TOM KELLY

Features

Frost at Midnight: The Poetry of Winter
Christopher James

Long before Robert Frost stopped by snowy woods on a snowy evening, winter had captured the poetical imagination of generations of writers. Associated with melancholy, beauty, desolation, isolation and introspection (stock in trade in other words to the penniless poet) perhaps this should come as no surprise. The winter poem is the staple of every poet from Shakespeare to Hardy; Emily Brontë to Simon Armitage. Tellingly, these poems are among the most compelling and enduring of their output.

Shakespeare often equated the moods of man with the seasons, from Richard's III's notorious declaration: 'Now is winter of our discontent' to the piteous cry in King Henry VI Part III : 'I that did never weep, now melt with woe / That winter should cut off our springtime so.' He uses winter here as a shorthand to describe the passing of joy, success, of youth, potency and promise. The pathetic fallacy of the natural world is a device used to elicit the reader's empathy and understanding. Shakespeare assumes we have a pre-existing well of physical and emotional connections with winter from which to draw. We know how winter *feels*, both on our skin and in our bones, but also its curious stultifying power over the mind.

When it comes to the poetry of winter, Coleridge's 'Frost at Midnight' sets the benchmark, an elegant meditation on a child's future by the fireside in the dead of winter. The opening lines skilfully establish the scene, creating a mood of silence and intimacy:

> The frost performs its secret ministry
> Unhelped by any wind

Through the use of personification and a quietly insistent sibilance (the repetition of the 's' and 'e' sound), the ice forming silently on the glass takes on a sacred, even magical quality. It is a reminder of the power and beauty of the natural world and the mystery of creation, all themes explored later in the poem. The poem becomes an incantation of sorts, and the speaker whispers a final blessing on the child he watches over: 'Therefore all seasons shall be sweet to thee,' going on to suggest that the secret ministry will 'hang' the 'eve-drop' in 'silent icicles / Quietly shining to the quiet Moon.' It is a winter prayer – portraying the sounds of winter as well as its stimulating affect on the mind; it is a season for reflection and rumination.

By contrast, William Blake takes a highly dramatic approach to the season. His poem To Winter (written around 1770) whips up storms that are 'unchained... for he has rear'd his sceptre over the world.' In this painterly, wildly imaginative work, Blake imparts his vision of a season which has its lair at the top of the world:

> The north is thine; there hast thou built thy dark
> Deep-founded habitation.

In a nightmarish turn, a beast emerges from this den:

> ....the direful monster whose skin clings
> To his strong bones, strides over the groaning rocks.

He wreaks havoc on the Earth; 'withers all in silence ... freezes up frail life.' But with the coming of spring 'heaven smiles' and 'the monster / Is driven yelling to his caves beneath Mount Hecla.' Drawing on folklore, specifically the fascinating superstition that a mountain in Iceland harbours the gates to hell, Blake creates a gothic fantasy to rival Mary's Shelley's Frankenstein.

Thomas Hardy is better known for his gloomy themes and vivid, but occasionally lumpen prose. Who could forget his bleak descriptions of the frost hardened fields in Tess of the D'Urbervilles? What a delight then, to stumble across his comic vignette Ice on the Highway. Based on a single fleeting image – 'Seven buxom women abreast, and arm in arm' as they teeter down an 'ice-bound road' – as warm hearted as the day is cold.

Their vitality ('breathing warm') solidarity and giddy *joi de vivre* at having to leave behind their 'lumbering van' is infectious. Just eleven lines long, as light as a snowflake and flawlessly capturing the novelty of a frosty day. With the merry prospect of 'the nearing Saturday night' ahead of them, Hardy is struck by their laughter as they stagger and slide.' The juxtaposition of the winter's day with their warmth of the women's friendship and strength of sprit is perfectly judged. Like the best poetry, the reader can inhabit the moment described, hearing and seeing every detail through the poet's eyes.

One can almost imagine Hardy himself standing watching, utterly captivated and charmed.

As icily beautiful as the snowbound Russian landscape she describes, Anna Akhmatova's Vorenezh is a gem of compression and atmospherics. The town 'is frozen solid in a vice/Trees, walls, snow beneath a glass.' The poet uses the winter imagery, and the prism of ice as a different way of looking at the world. It also becomes a way of seeing into the past, where 'the field of heroes lingers in my thought/Kulikovo's barbarian battlefield.' Just as the town is dressed in a ghostly white, it is haunted by history. Winter's power to transform a landscape is equal to that of language itself: the 'frozen poplars' are 'like glasses for a toast.'

Paul Farley uses similar devices in his devastating poem, 11th February 1963, the date both of Sylvia Plath's suicide and the recording of The Beatles first LP. Notoriously it was 'the worst winter for decades' and the bleak, numbing cold is somehow an appropriate setting for Plath's senseless end. In breathtaking style he takes us back with him in time, as if going deep beneath the snow: '…think until you're many Februaries/deep in thought with me,' creating a tone of intimacy, similar to Coleridge's. He invites us to concentrate until we 'find London/on that day as held inside a glacier.' It is a thrilling conceit, that a day, a memory, a moment can be perfectly preserved like a mammoth beneath layers of snow. London is almost like a snow globe, John Lennon laying down Twist and Shout with all the promise of new decade, while the most gifted poet of her generation loses her life. Winter, Farley seems to argue, does strange things to the mind, distorting time and reality.

In his early poem Snow Joke, Simon Armitage deploys his trade mark black humour and colloquial style. 'Heard the one about the guy from Heaton Mersey?' it begins. It unfolds into an alternative Winter's Tale featuring a flash, unlikeable man with a 'wife at home, lover in Hyde, mistress/in Newton-le-Willows' who comes a cropper when he 'snubbed the police warning-light' and tries to make it back through a blizzard. Relayed in the manner of a pub anecdote, it's brilliantly conversational, mimicking the callous glee of the pub bore with a new story up his sleeve; he's more interested in relaying the macabre detail than sharing any sympathy for the man.

Here the snow is the silent killer, deceptively serene as the man slowly freezes to death; who:

81

watched the windscreen filling up

with snow, and it felt good, and the whisky
from his hip-flask warm and smooth.

The jokey tone and startling detail only serve to accentuate the true horror
as:

They found him slumped against the steering wheel
with VOLVO printed backwards in his frozen brow.

The pay-off is equally vivid, an exceptionally well-conceived simile relaying
how the passer by:

...heard the horn, moaning
softly like an alarm clock under an eiderdown.

It is a droll answer to the trite snow poem, wonderfully revealing the brutal
heart of middle England.

In a sense, the numbing beauty of the snow on the windscreen brings us full
circle back to Robert Frost, who watches, in a similarly hypnotic state: 'his
woods fill up with snow'. Yes, winter offers a luminous vision of a world
renewed and purified. But there is a darkness too — the beauty is not to be
trusted; it conceals the power of death over life and its charms are to be
treated with caution. They are to be admired, but ultimately resisted:

The woods are lovely, dark and deep
But I have promises to keep
And miles to go before I sleep
And miles to go before I sleep.

*Christopher James won first prize in the National Poetry Competition 2008. His most
recent collection is* The Fool *(Templar, 2014).*

In The Snug with Ian Harker

Tom Weir

Tom Weir's iOTA Shot Pamphlet is *The Outsider* **and was followed by his first collection** *All that Falling,* **both launched at Templar's Keats House Readings and the Derwent Poetry Festival.**

When did you first realise that such a thing as poetry existed?

I was quite old really; I used to listen to music a lot, and the music I liked was with really good lyricists like Leonard Cohen and Bob Dylan, and I used to take the words out and use the rhythm of the song, so I used to write loads in my teenage years, but instead of learning about poetry I'd just use their rhythms but write it on the page as poetry. Unless you count primary school, when I was obsessed with a poem by Roger McGough called 'The Footy Poem'. And when I was at 6th form college I went and heard Benjamin Zephaniah and loved it. I suppose I've always been aware of it but didn't know how to write it.

So, when you first read formal poetry — was that after your undergraduate degree?

No, it was during the first year. A tutor there said my writing was like poetry and she told me to study poetry and invited me to one of her workshops. And she made it really fun and inspiring and played archive recordings of poets and introduced us to the Beats, who I'd never heard of. She told us about Allan Ginsberg and the boxingring battles and stuff like that. She started giving me books and recommending books to read and she gave us writing exercises. The poetry I wrote was fucking terrible! She still takes the piss out of me now for how bad it was at the start.

What was your degree?

Creative Arts. It was half writing and half visual arts and within that I got to study units like life writing and narrative non-fiction and one of the modules within that was poetry.

'I felt ...freer writing poetry for the art tutors than..the poetry tutors – the art side offered much looser creativity; they allowed us to experiment...

So, you stumbled across it?

Yeah, I was really bad at drawing, so I had to find other ways to make art. I felt a lot freer writing poetry for the art tutors than I did for the poetry tutors – the art side offered much looser creativity; they allowed us to experiment. My photography tutor was really into poetry and he would give us books to read that weren't quite the same as the ones we were given on the poetry course. He was really into French poetry and its links to artistic movements and really encouraged poetry within visual art, so my project would be to document a trip and make art out of it. It sounds pretentious, but that's where I enjoyed writing the most.

You started off with travel writing. That's a strong element in your pamphlet and your full collection.

Yeah, I always travelled a lot when I was little, and I obsessively kept a journal and a diary; even before I started writing poetry I was always writing on notepads and I did the same at uni. Then I decided to go back to Vietnam and live there rather than just travel.

'There are only so many poems you can write about shopping and Sainsbury's ...I needed to have something to write about...

You did a Master's straight after your undergraduate degree?

Yeah. I went to uni quite late, did a Master's straight after, and then needed to get away. There are only so many poems you can write about shopping and Sainsbury's and I needed to have something to write about. I need to experience something to write about it, and I felt the need to shake things up a bit. I was in Bath for four years. It's a nice place for a couple of years, but it got a bit stagnant for me so I just needed to go away and write independently – not for a course or for the approval of any particular tutor; I wanted to revisit the world of poetry on my own terms.

What was the gap between coming back to the UK and your pamphlet coming out – what happened in between?

Very little, really. I started sending off poems, I loved the rejections even, I loved the fact that I was actually communicating with someone that I didn't know. So after uni. I didn't write for a long time, I'd got a bit of burnout, and it took me a couple of years before I started to send stuff off. About five years after I came back from teaching abroad I started putting work together – quite intensely, really, for a year or so. Then I sent off to Templar about five to midnight on the day of the deadline, got a phone call a few weeks later saying I'd won. I think I need deadlines to work to. So the minute I had a deadline I started to write a lot more than I had been previously.

'...poems were battling against each other to get into the book. Poems went in then got taken out, then they were in again...

With the book, you knew what you chose was going to be published – did that make it a different process from submitting a pamphlet to a competition?

Definitely. With the full collection there was a lovely obsessive dilemma – I'm really indecisive anyway, but I was changing it a lot and it encouraged me to work really hard on certain poems and mould

85

them and improve them and it was like the poems were battling against each other to get into the book. Poems went in then got taken out, then they were in again, then they were out, and some to this day I still think would have been better than others.

' ...there's only so many times you can stand up and read poems for fifteen minutes about sheep and cows and rambling countryside...

You only find out what a poem's actually worth when you read it to other people or when other people read it; that's when it's really alive.

Yeah. I learned a lot when the pamphlet came out and I took it to readings. I noticed that what I was writing needed shaking up. When I was reading just from the pamphlet I got tired of it quite quickly, and I became aware of the need to change gear. Within a block of work there's only so many times you can stand up and read poems for fifteen minutes about sheep and cows and rambling countryside. Reading to other people you find out what they like and respond to and you're almost editing as you are reading – if they go well together at readings they might sit well in a book.

' It's not unusual for me to write fifteen of sixteen drafts of the same poem...

There are two straw men in poetry – that poetry happens as a result of god-like inspiration – we still have a cult of the genius poet. The opposite side of that is that poetry is just hard graft and all you have to do is work and work and work and it'll come. Where do you put yourself on that spectrum?

I can't have one without the other. I can't sit down and say Now I'm going to write a really good poem. There needs to be a balance. I won't write without there being a good reason to write. Some poems have taken me more than a year to finish, but without the initial idea –

the thing that's got me excited – the poem's not there. It's not unusual for me to write fifteen of sixteen drafts of the same poem, so one isn't possible without the other. I don't like reading a poem where I feel like it's a poem that someone's written because they wanted to write a poem rather than they wrote it because they needed to say something. I can't be bothered with poetry written by someone that's never lived something, never experienced something, but has sat down with loads of research and decided to write a poem about it. Personally I couldn't write a poem like that; but at the same time I couldn't write a good poem without hours and hours of obsessive tinkering. Yeah, I'm in between.

'It's very difficult to get published, and not just for somebody who's starting out – even established writers are struggling...

So you're a 'five'.

Yes, I'm a five. I used to hear other people talk like this about poetry and think – that's bollocks. Although there are certain poems...I'm getting more of an instinct, and I know when some poems are best left and I know they're going to be poems but I don't have to force them – I just want them to be there. I don't think I've ever written a first draft and thought – brilliant, that's finished. I need to write a lot of crap and then pick from that what I want to use and then concentrate on it.

'It's hard to justify, your saying that you're just going to sit down at a table on your own and write with everyone saying – let's do this, let's do that...

It's very difficult to get published, and not just for somebody who's starting out – even established writers are struggling, for several reasons. Was there ever a point when you felt 'I'm never going to get published', and how did you deal with that? What made you keep on trying? I didn't, to be honest; I didn't keep on, I totally stopped submitting. I submitted to magazines and journals, but only to a select few, I got lovely rejection letters; felt great about how nice they were about my writing, but then thought it was time to stop, because I thought I was never going to succeed. But I continued to enter pamphlet competitions, the iOTA Shot competition along with a couple of others – then all of a sudden I won the Book & Pamphlet award and then the National Poetry Competition which I entered instead of submitting to a magazine – I got highly commended in that.

I think the confidence thing is big with me: it's hard to justify writing if you're not getting published. You need to have the confidence to sit down and write, however you find that – without it you're not going to sit down and write because you feel silly doing it. It's hard to justify, your saying that you're just going to sit down at a table on your own and write with everyone saying – let's do this, let's do that – until you start having a bit of success first. It gets harder and harder to justify doing that without feeling a bit stupid. And then the minute you do get a bit of success it allows you to say – I need to do some writing or I need to do some editing and I'm just going to spend a couple of hours doing that, and then nobody looks at you like they would if you had never got anything published.

What did you last read that got you really excited?

Bloody hell, there's a question! There's people I always read and enjoy reading whenever I've left it too long. There are poems that I get very excited about reading – I've recently read a bit of Cousin Coat by Sean O'Brien, I found a few poems in there that I loved. Gerard Woodward I always go back to; I love his stuff. Don Paterson. I rarely sit there now with a full collection: I've got loads of books and if I'm going to sit and read for the evening I won't read a collection, I'll grab four or five books and then flick through each one and pick out different poems. I'm reading a bit less these days which is why I'm probably writing a bit less.

'**You need to have the confidence to sit down and write...**